Lydia Crook

TWO PLAYER BIG FUN BOOK

Ivy Kids

KT-459-960

HOW TO USE THIS BOOK

The **Two Player Big Fun Book** is packed with fun things for a pair of pals.

For some activities you will work together as a team. For others, you are in competition!

Fun this **B I G** can't all fit the same way up likein a normal book, though. You'll need to move the book around and change where you're sitting for each activity — depending on which way up the text is.

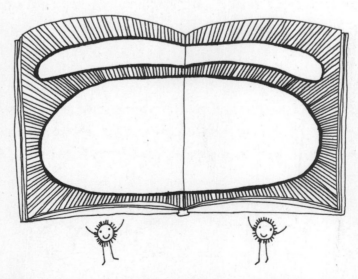

Sometimes you'll sit alongside each other . . .

This book belongs to

Hold this page up to a mirror and then write your names below (but the writing has to be back-to-front, too).

and

First published in the UK in 2014 by

Ivy Press

210 High Street

Lewes

East Sussex BN7 2NS

United Kingdom

www.ivypress.co.uk.

Copyright © 2014 Ivy Press Limited

All rights reserved. No part of this
book may be reproduced or transmitted
in any form or by any means, electronic
or mechanical, including photocopying,
recording, or by any information
storage-and-retrieval system, without
written permission from the copyright holder.

ISBN: 978-1-78240-142-1

This book was conceived, designed and produced by

Ivy Press

CREATIVE DIRECTOR   Peter Bridgewater
COMMISSIONING EDITOR   Georgia Amson-Bradshaw
MANAGING EDITOR   Hazel Songhurst
ART DIRECTOR   Kim Hankinson
DESIGNER & ILLUSTRATOR   Lydia Crook

Printed in China

Origination by Ivy Press Reprographics

10 9 8 7 6 5 4 3 2 1

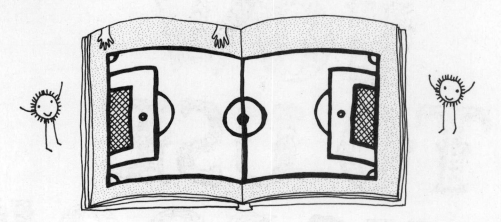

. . . other times you'll sit opposite each other, with the book in between.

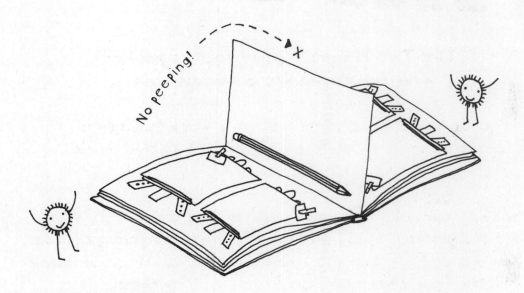

No peeping!

Some activities have a 'screen' page for you to hold up in the middle. This is to prevent peeping while the game is underway!

Most of the games appear more than once. Take turns in going first, so you both have the chance to do everything, and get an equal share of the Big Fun.

Woo hoo!

THE FIEND

How to play the fiendish maze . . .
Face each other at opposite sides of the book. See which player can get through the maze on their page to reach the centre first.

PLAY
SQUARES
ON THIS PAGE

→

How to play . . .

Take turns to draw a single line to join any two dots that are next to each other on the grid. The lines can join the dots horizontally or vertically (but not diagonally).

The player who draws the line that completes one square earns one point, and gets another turn. Put your initials in that square.

The game ends when no more lines can be drawn -- the player with the most points wins!

The steps below show one square being made. Player 'B' drew the final line in the square, so they get that point.

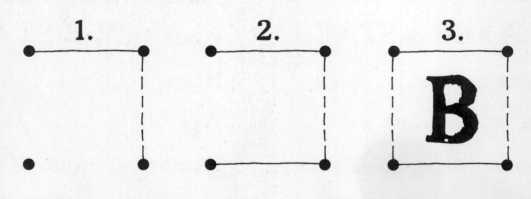

1.   2.   3.

B

—— Player A   - - - Player B

PLAYER 1 STATS

Name _ _ _ _ _ _ _ _ _ _ _ _

Age _ _ _ _ _ _ _ _ _ _ _ _

Number of squares won

_ _ _ _ _ _ _ _ _ _ _ _ _

PLAYER 2 STATS

Name _ _ _ _ _ _ _ _ _ _ _ _

Age _ _ _ _ _ _ _ _ _ _ _ _

Number of squares won

_ _ _ _ _ _ _ _ _ _ _ _ _

The winner was _ _ _ _ _ _ _ _ _ _ _ _ with _ _ _ squares.

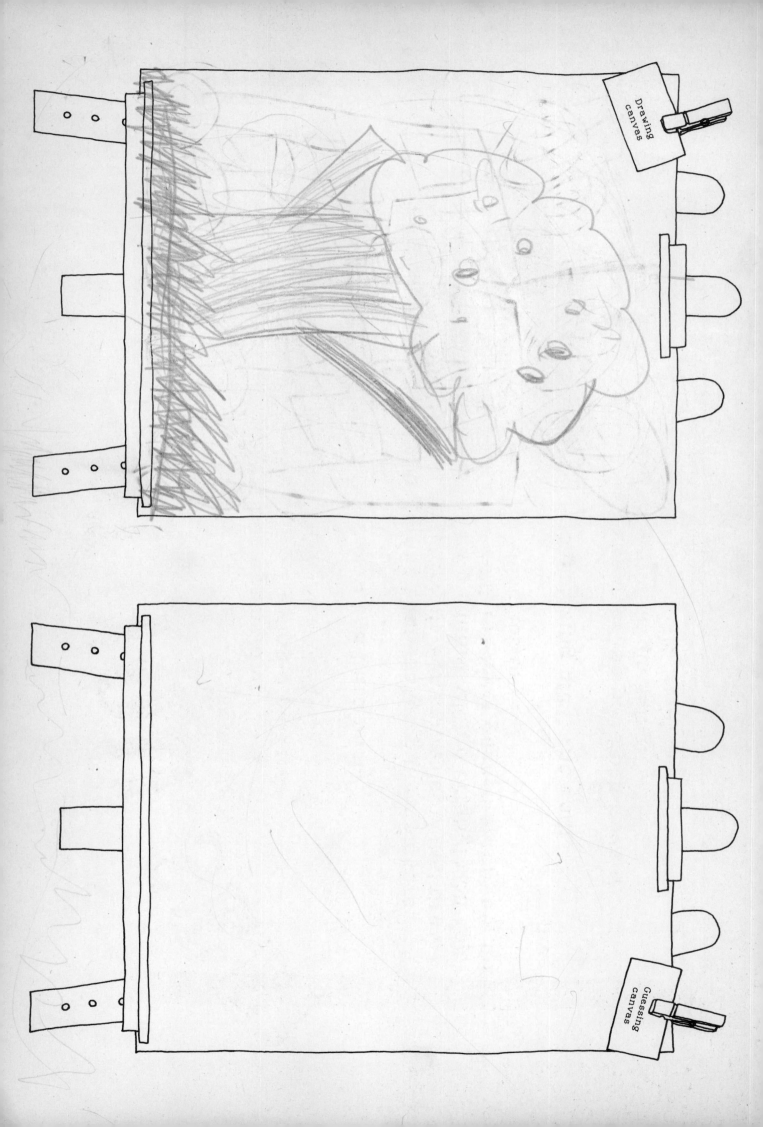

SAY WHAT YOU SEE

With this page held up,
player 1 starts by drawing a picture
on their drawing canvas.

Good work – but now the hard part!

Describe the shapes and lines that make up your picture,
without saying what you have drawn. For example, if you drew
a house you could describe it as a square with a triangle on top.
Player 2 must try to draw a copy of it on their guessing canvas, just
from the description.

No questions, and no guessing until the end!

Once you've finished, swap over, so you both have a
go at drawing and at guessing.

SAY WHAT YOU SEE!

With this page held up, player 1 starts by drawing a picture on their drawing canvas.

Good work – but now the hard part!

Describe the shapes and lines that make up your picture, without saying what you have drawn. For example, if you drew a house you could describe it as a square with a triangle on top. Player 2 must try to draw a copy of it on their guessing canvas, just from the description.

No questions, and no guessing until the end!

Once you've finished, swap over, so you both have a go at drawing and at guessing.

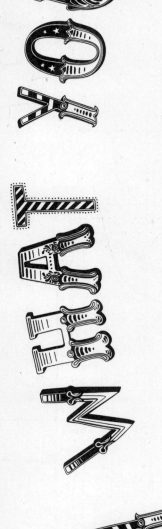

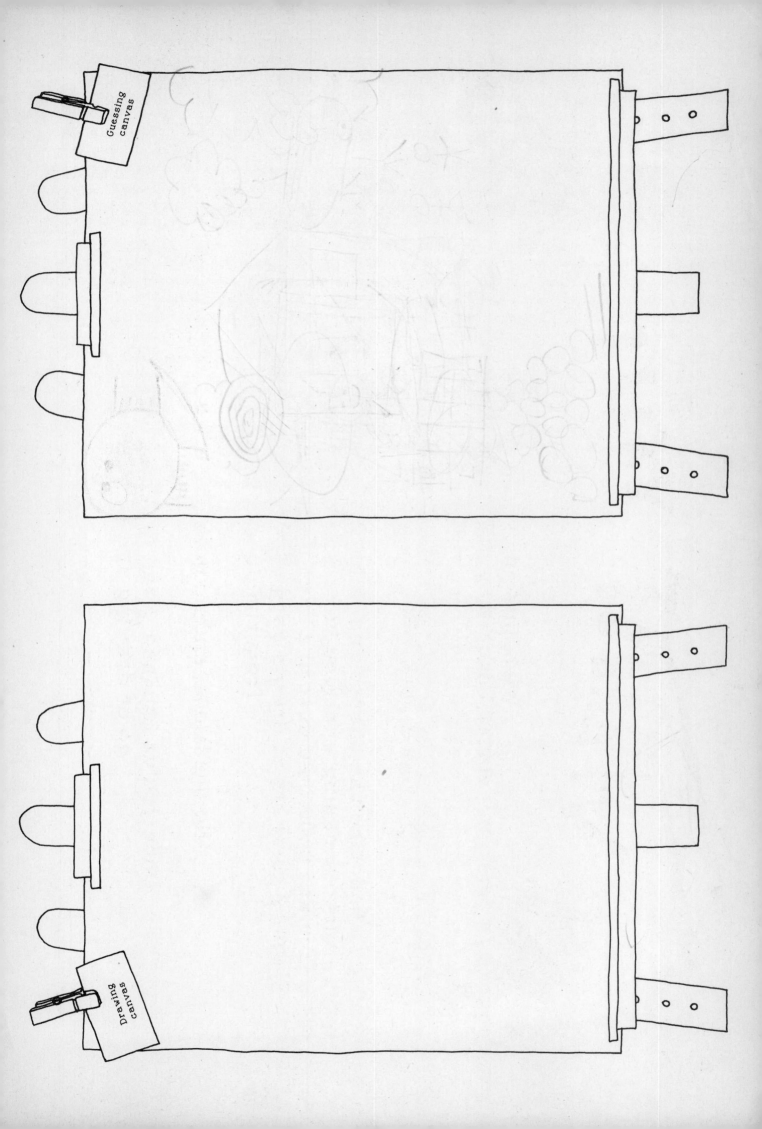

WHAT'S THE STORY?

PLAYER 1'S STORY

1 " .... !!" she shouted, while she

2 .... the 3 ....

She was taking her 4 ....

5 .... to the vet because he had a sore

.... pet

6 .... , but her car had broken down

on the way, so they both had to

7 .... there, 8 ....

....

WORD KEY:

1. Exclamation!   3. Noun   5. Noun   7. Verb
2. Verb (past tense) 4. Adjective   6. Noun   8. Adverb (ending . . . ly)

HOW IT WORKS...

Read through your story (silently!), and ask the other player for words to fill in the gaps (clues on the types of words you need are provided). Once you've both filled in all the gaps, take turns to read your story aloud, and see whose is the funniest.

WORD TYPES

VERB - a doing word - walk, cook, jump...
NOUN - a naming word - house, giraffe, river...
ADJECTIVE - a describing word - green, tall, strange...
ADVERB - describes the way an action happens - slowly, completely, gently...
EXCLAMATION - a short utterance - Gosh! Hurrah! Cripes!

PLAYER 2'S STORY

Wesley was learning to play the 1 .... , but was progressing 2 .... because he had to use his 3 .... Sometimes his pet 4 .... tried to help, but wasn't very good because its fringe was too 5 .... After lots of time spent 6 .... , they both felt 7 .... with their 8 ....

WORD KEY:

1. Noun

2. Adverb (ending ...ly)

3. Noun

4. Noun

5. Adjective

6. Verb (ending ...ing)

7. Noun (emotion)

8. Noun

Mandalas are beautiful, detailed patterns and you can create two here. They've been started for you. You can both draw at the same time — add something to your own pattern, then swap sides and add something to each other's. You could draw a decorative ring each time and add dots, shapes, swirls, squiggles — anything you like!

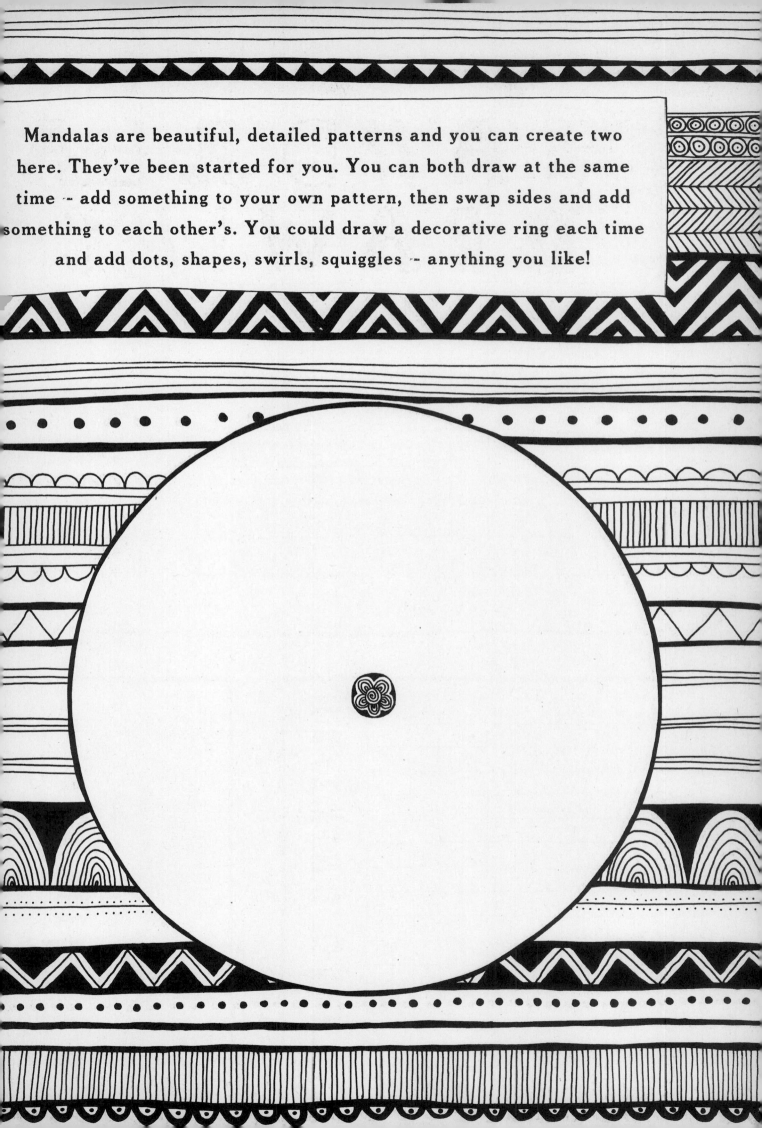

MAIN GRID

Draw your fleet on this grid.

	1	2	3	4	5	6	7	8	9	10	11	12
A												
B												
C												
D												
E												
F												
G												
H												
I												
J												
K												
L												

YOUR FLEET

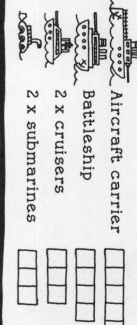

Aircraft carrier

Battleship

2 x cruisers

2 x submarines

TRACKING GRID

	1	2	3	4	5	6	7	8	9	10	11	12
A												
B												
C												
D												
E												
F												
G												
H												
I												
J												
K												
L												

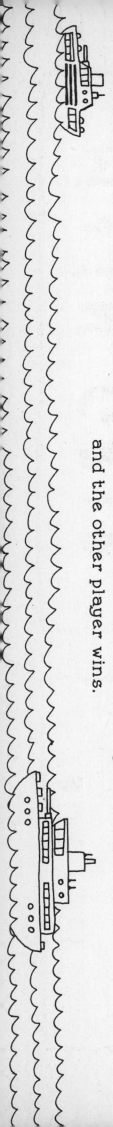

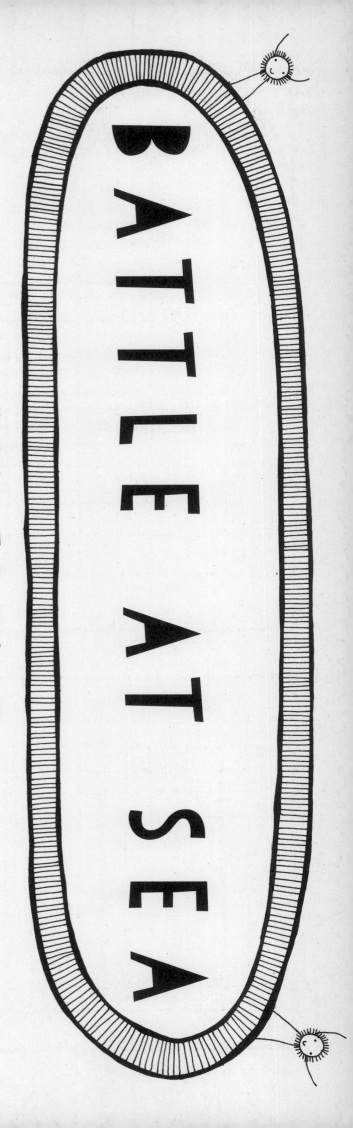

BATTLE AT SEA

HOW TO PLAY . . .

Sit facing each other, then hold this page up in the middle.

Choose where you want to place each boat in your fleet. Shade in the correct number of squares on the main grid for each boat, then you're ready to play.

Take turns in calling out a square from the grid (A3, D5, etc). The other player then looks at their grid and tells you if they have a boat on that square. If the answer is yes – you've got a hit! Mark hits with a cross on your tracking grid, and misses with a dash.
This will help you build a picture of where the other player's fleet is.

Once you've guessed all of the squares taken up by one boat, you have SUNK THE BATTLESHIP!
When all of one player's boats have been sunk, the game is over
and the other player wins.

BATTLE AT SEA

HOW TO PLAY . . . .

Sit facing each other, then hold this page up in the middle.

Choose where you want to place each boat in your fleet. Shade in the correct number of squares on the main grid for each boat, then you're ready to play.

Take turns in calling out a square from the grid (A3, D5, etc). The other player then looks at their grid and tells you if they have a boat on that square. If the answer is yes – you've got a hit! Mark hits with a cross on your tracking grid, and misses with a dash. This will help you build a picture of where the other player's fleet is.

Once you've guessed all of the squares taken up by one boat, you have SUNK THE BATTLESHIP! When all of one player's boats have been sunk, the game is over and the other player wins.

YOUR FLEET

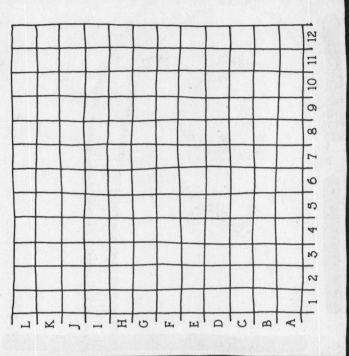

Aircraft carrier
Battleship
2 x cruisers
2 x submarines

MAIN GRID

Draw your fleet on this grid.

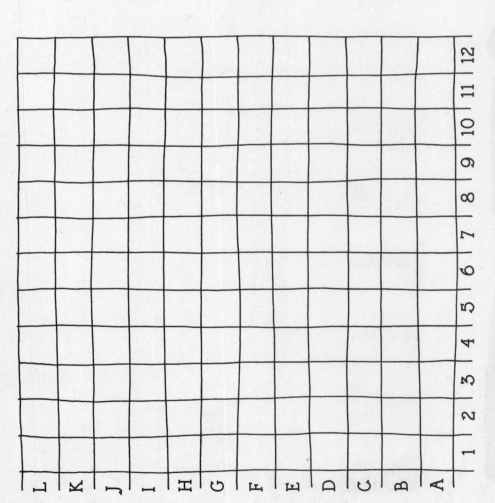

TRACKING GRID

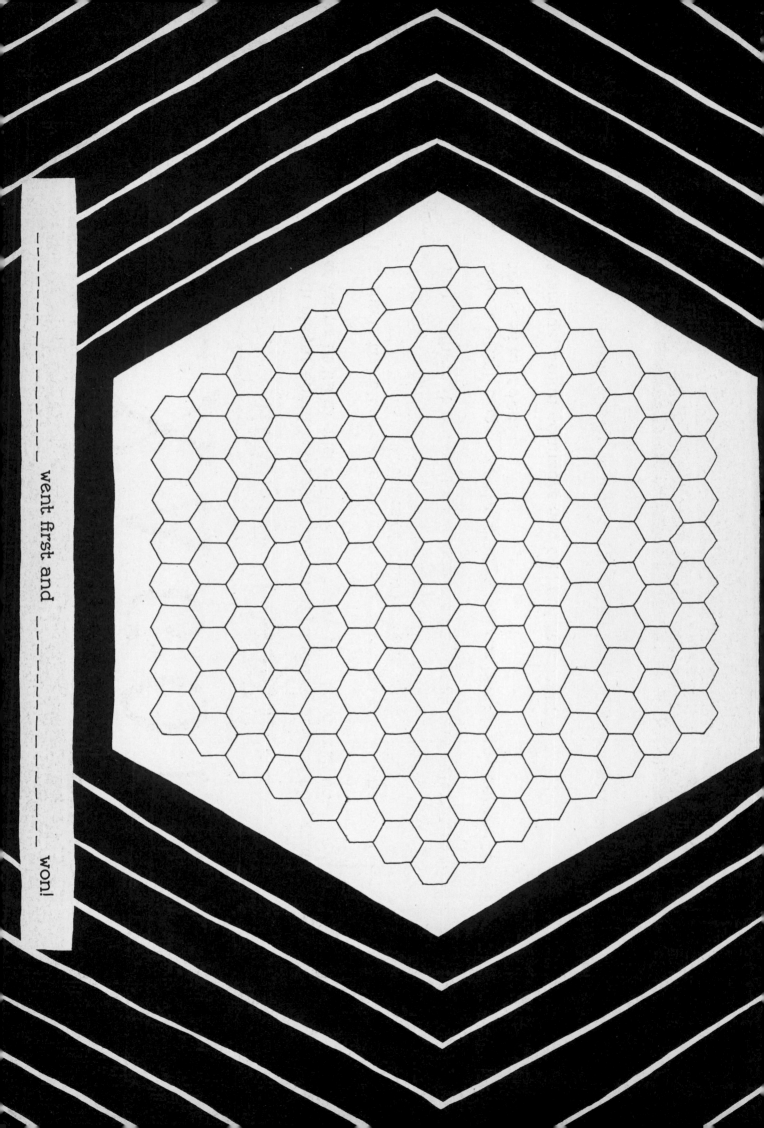

went first and _____ won!

HEXAGONS

HOW TO PLAY . . .

Each player should choose a coloured pencil to use for the game.
Take turns to fill in one 'cell' of the board at a time with your colour.

The aim is to colour cells next to each other to create one of three types of connection:

1. A ring, which is a continuous loop with at least one cell in the middle.

2. A fork, which connects three edges of the board (the corners don't count as an edge).

3. A bridge, which connects any two of the corners.

The first player to make any of these connections wins!

MY SCORE WAS:

MY LIST OF WORDS FOUND:

HOW TO PLAY:

With this page held up, the first player calls a letter, then both players write that letter in a square on their grid. Take turns calling out letters and writing them down, until your grids are full. The aim is to arrange the letters as you write them down to make as many words as possible.

Once the grids are full, write down all the words you can find. You get points for words in a vertical or horizontal row (not diagonals). You also get points for words within words - so if you found 'train', you'd also get points for 'rain' and 'in'.

5-letter word - Whew, well done! 10 points!
4-letter word - Good effort, have 5 points.
3-letter word - Not bad, have 2 points.
2-letter word - OK, you can have 1 point.

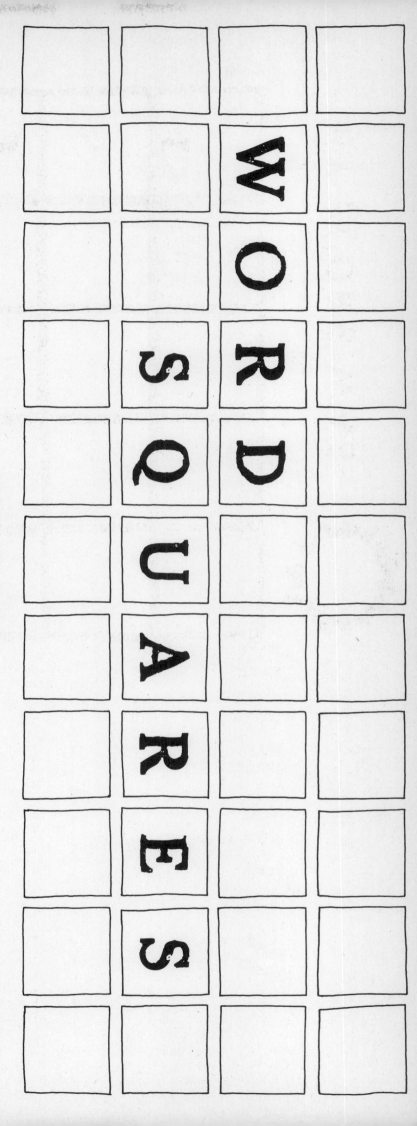

W O R D S
Q U A R E S

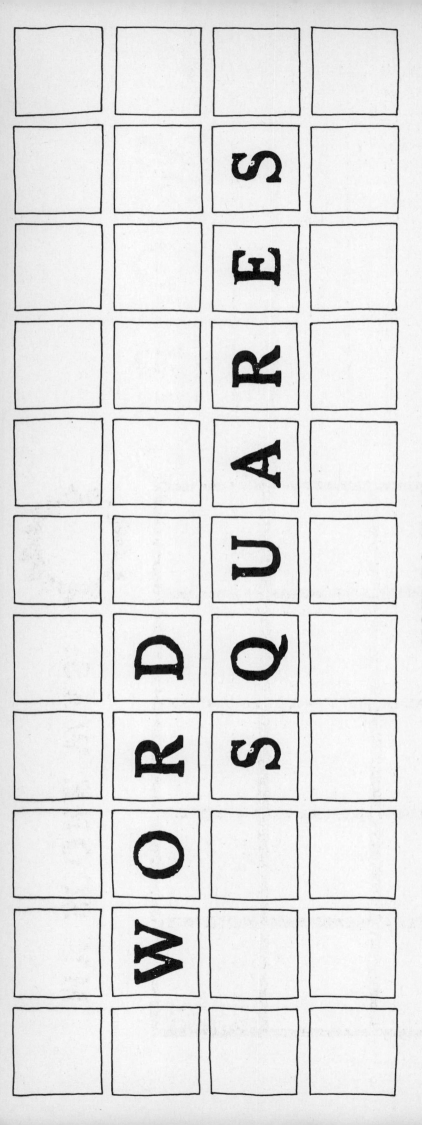

HOW TO PLAY:

With this page held up, the first player calls out a letter, then both players write that letter in a square on their grid. Take turns calling out letters and writing them down, until your grids are full. The aim is to arrange the letters as you write them down to make as many words as possible.

Once the grids are full, write down all the words you can find.

You get points for words in a vertical or horizontal row (not diagonals). You also get points for words within words -- so if you found 'train', you'd also get points for 'rain' and 'in'.

5-letter word -- Whew, well done! 10 points!
4-letter word -- Good effort, have 5 points.
3-letter word -- Not bad, have 2 points.
2-letter word -- OK, you can have 1 point.

MY SCORE WAS:

SQUIGG

Sometimes, starting a drawing is the hardest part. Luckily, you can help each other out! Each player should quickly do a small squiggle in the middle of their frame, then turn the book around.

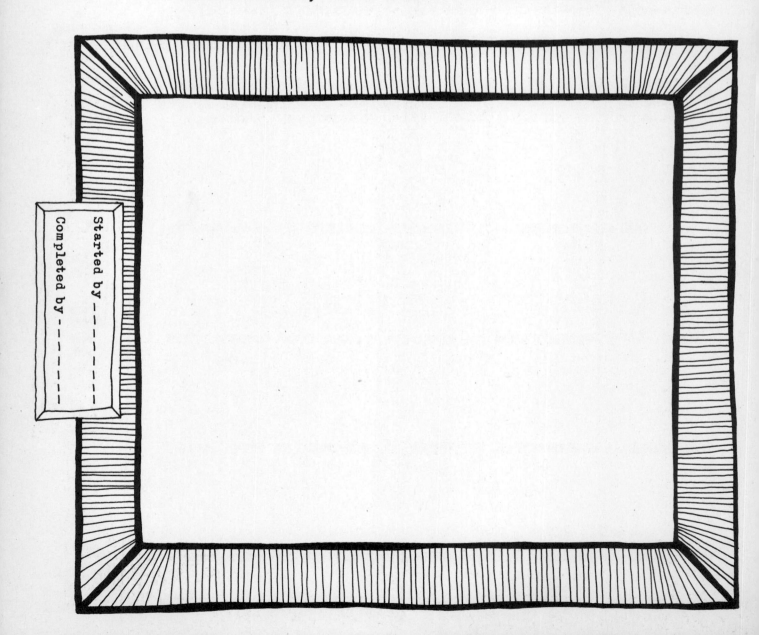

Started by ----------
Completed by ----------

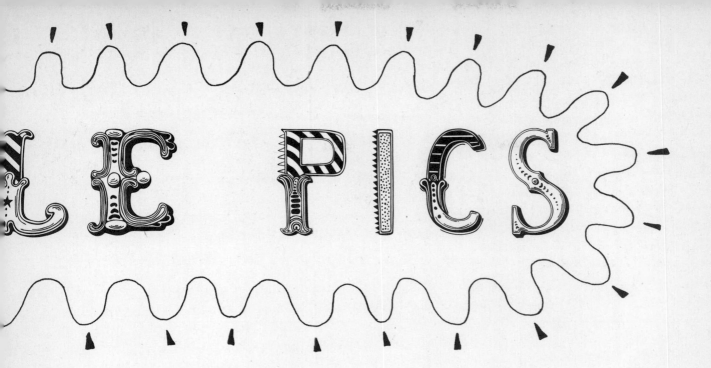

LE PICS

Now your drawing has been started for you, decide what you think it looks like and add details to turn it into a complete picture!

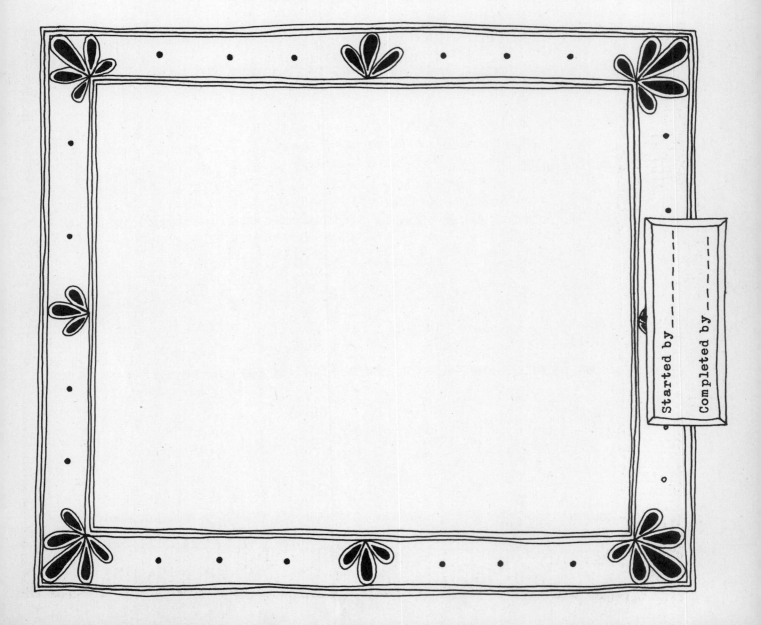

Started by _ _ _ _ _ _

Completed by _ _ _ _ _ _

MY TOTAL CATEGORIES SCORE WAS: _ _ _ _ _ _

	FRUITS	ANIMALS	COUNTRIES	CARTOONS	FILMS
G					
L					
O					
V					
E					

CATEGORIES

How does it work?

Hold up this page, set a timer for four minutes – then you're ready to start!

In each square of your grid, write a word that fits under the category at the top of the column, and starts with the letter at the beginning of the row.

The game is finished either when the time is up or when one player fills their grid.

Compare your answers and make sure you agree all the words are OK (no made-up words!).

You get no points for words that you and the other player both wrote down, but one point per word that only you thought of. If you filled the whole grid, you get five bonus points!

The player with the most points wins.

Ready, steady, go . . .

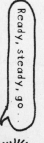

CATEGORIES

How does it work?

Hold up this page, set a timer for four minutes – then you're ready to start!

In each square of your grid, write a word that fits under the category at the top of the column, and starts with the letter at the beginning of the row.

The game is finished either when the time is up or when one player fills their grid.

Compare your answers and make sure you agree all the words are OK (no made-up words!).

You get no points for words that you and the other player both wrote down, but one point per word that only you thought of. If you filled the whole grid, you get five bonus points!

The player with the most points wins.

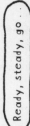

Ready, steady, go...

FRUITS	ANIMALS	COUNTRIES	CARTOONS	FILMS
G				
L				
O				
V				
E				

MY TOTAL CATEGORIES SCORE WAS: _ _ _ _ _

TAG-TEAM DRAWING

Work together to create a unique masterpiece, with a spot of tag-team drawing . . .
Player 1 does a quick doodle, then rotates the paper 90 degrees. Now it's player 2's turn.
"TAG!" Player 2 quickly adds to the doodle, then rotates the paper another 90 degrees.
Keep taking turns until the picture is complete - voila!

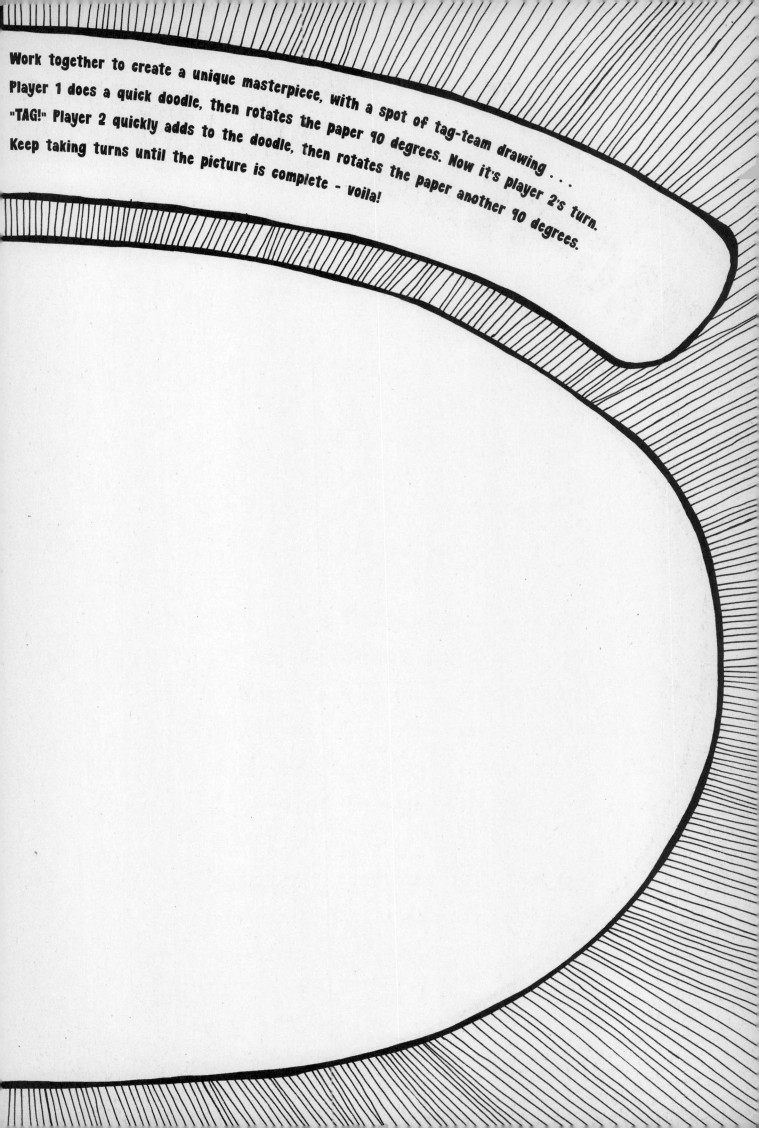

PIPE

HOW TO PLAY:

One player plays with black dots, the other plays with white dots.

Take turns connecting your dots, one line at a time. You can connect up or across (not diagonally), and you can only connect dots of your own colour. You cannot cross a line that has already been drawn.

The aim is to connect the dots in your colour to make a continuous line (or pipe) between the shorter sides of your grid.

LAYER

- ● Black dot player's name _____

- ○ White dot player's name _____

◄ – – – – – White dot player joins side to side – – ►

▲ – – – Black dot player joins up or down – – – – ►

The winner was _____

SPOT THE DIFFERENCES RACE

Hold this page up — and no peeking!

Race each other to find the ten differences between these pictures — circle them as you find them. The first player to find all ten, wins.

SPOT THE DIFFFERENCES RACE ⟶

Race each other to find the ten differences between these pictures — circle them as you find them.

The first player to find all ten, wins.

Hold this page up — and no peeking!

PICTURE

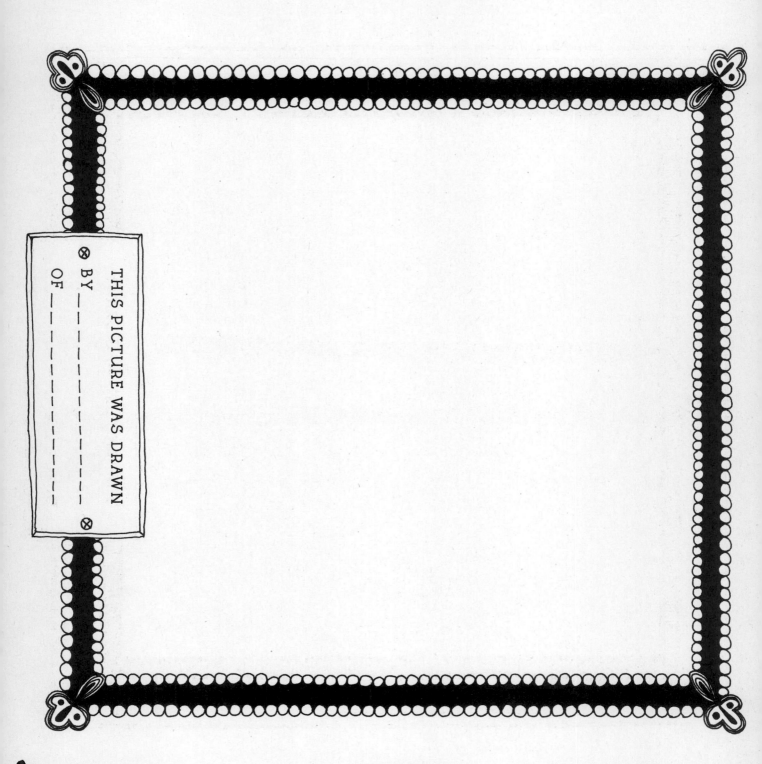

THIS PICTURE WAS DRAWN

⊗ BY _____

OF _____

THE GAME
Sitting at opposite ends of the book, draw a portrait of each other in the picture frame. Sounds easy enough, right?
WELL, there is a twist...
You must NOT look down at your drawing, you can ONLY look straight ahead at the person you are drawing!!

PERFECT

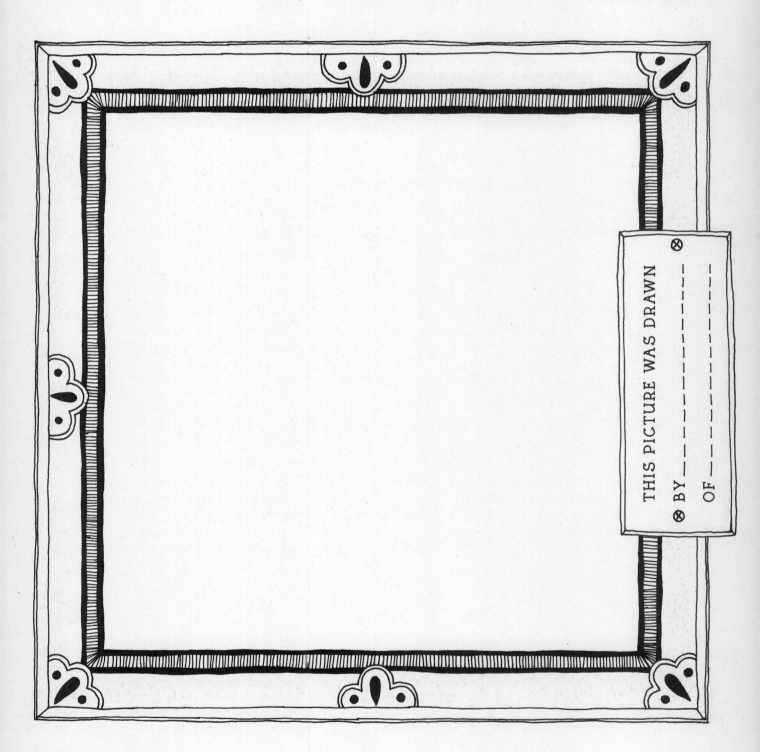

THIS PICTURE WAS DRAWN

⊗ BY — — — — — — —

OF — — — — — — —

When you have finished you can look at your portraits. Beautiful!
Optional rule: make it doubly exciting by playing against the clock
- try to complete your portraits in 30 seconds!

SPROUTS

Sprouts is like a game of dot-to-dots, but with a twist . . .

 > Here's how it works: <

Starting with the three dots on the opposite page, take turns to draw a line to connect two dots (or the line may start and end on the same dot). You should also draw a new dot somewhere on your new line.

Lines cannot cross, and each dot can only have three lines sprouting out of it. Eventually, it will become impossible to draw a new line without crossing an existing one – the last player to draw a line wins!

Here's an example of a two dot game :

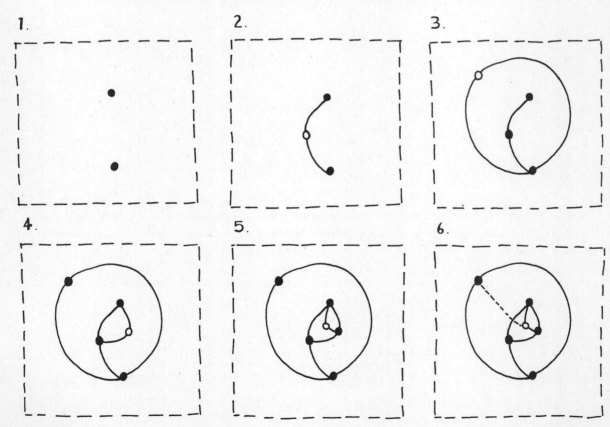

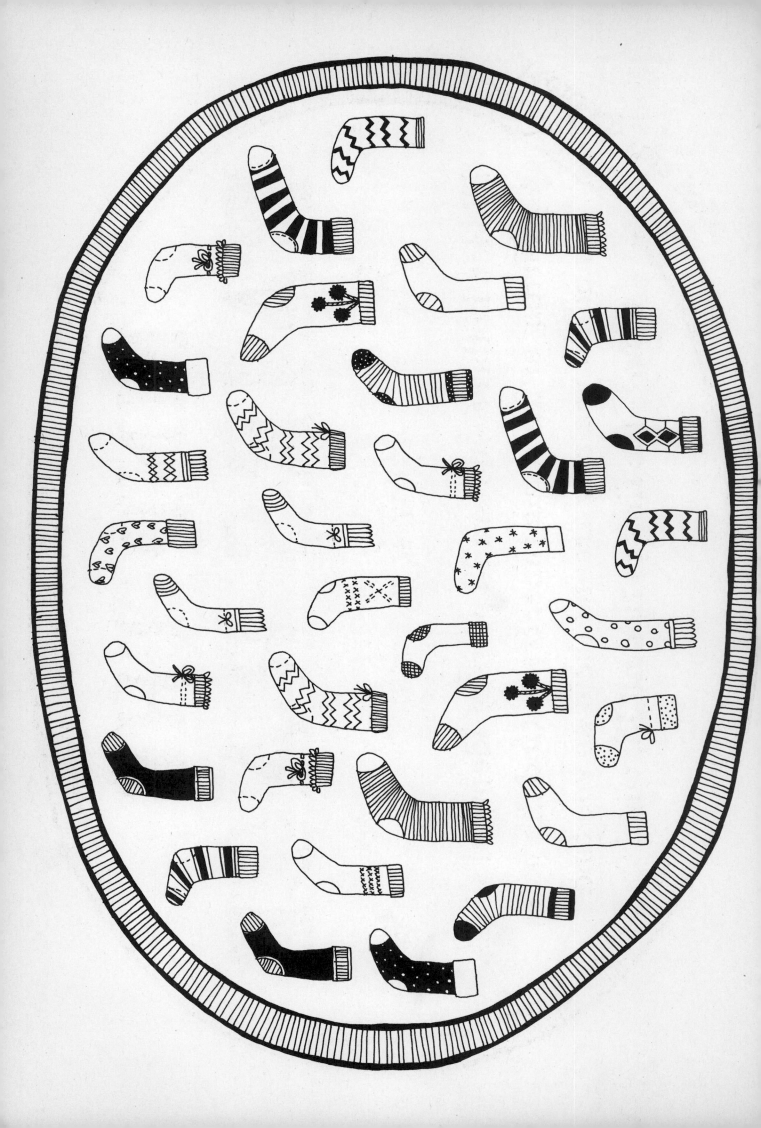

FIND THE PAIRS RACE

How it works:

Hidden in this scene are 13 pairs of identical socks.

Starting at the same time, try to find the pairs and draw a ring around them as you find them – the first to find all 13, wins!

Hold up this page.

FIND THE PAIRS RACE

How it works:

Hidden in this scene are 13 pairs of identical socks.

Starting at the same time, try to find the pairs and draw a ring around them as you find them -- the first to find all 13, wins!

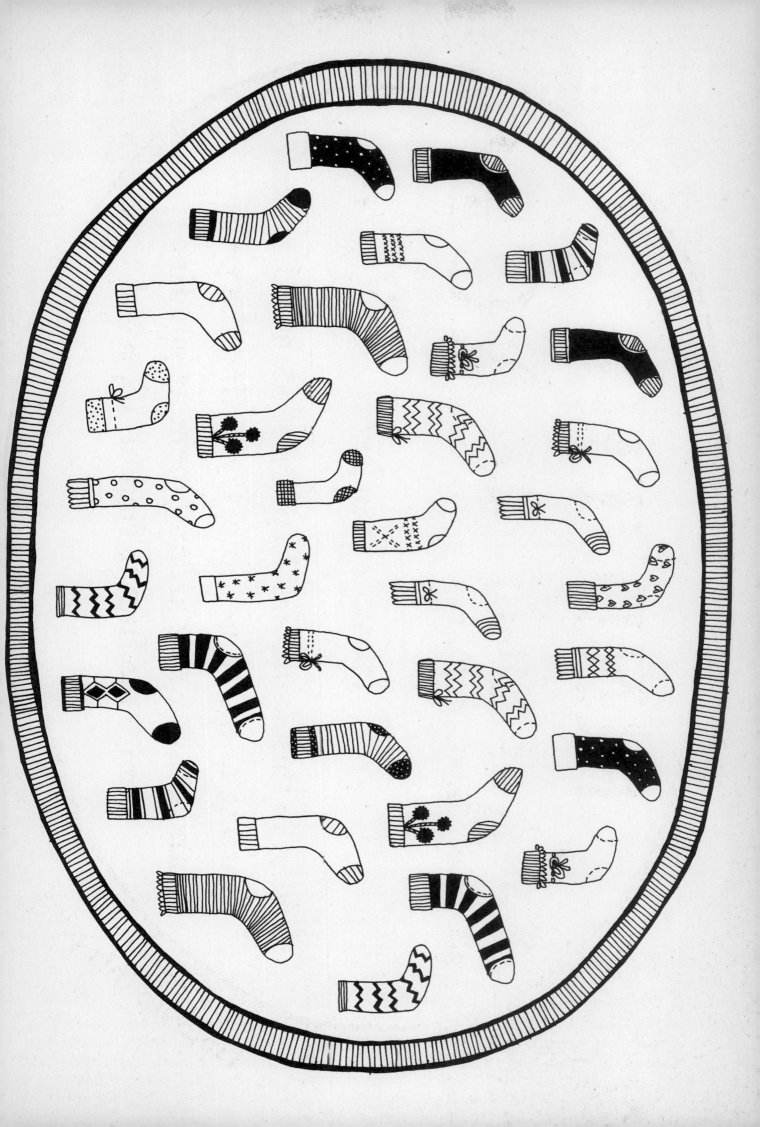

MIRROR DRAWING

drew this picture

WHAT TO DO:
Facing each other, pick one player to be lead artist and one to be their student. The artist begins drawing a beautiful scene in their picture frame. The student must try to exactly mirror what the lead artist is drawing — at the same time... Try to keep up!

MIRROR DRAWING

drew this picture

WHAT TO DO:

Facing each other, pick one player to be lead artist and one to be their
student. The artist begins drawing a beautiful scene in their picture
frame. The student must try to exactly mirror what the lead artist is
drawing – at the same time... Try to keep up!

FINGER

PLAYER 1 GOAL

PENALTY SHOOT-OUT

Make a football with a scrumpled up bit of paper: old receipts are perfect.
Take turns to place the ball on the 'O' in your penalty box and 'kick' it at the
opponent's goal, using your first finger and middle finger like a pair of legs.
You may draw football shoes onto your fingertips if you like.

FOOTBALL

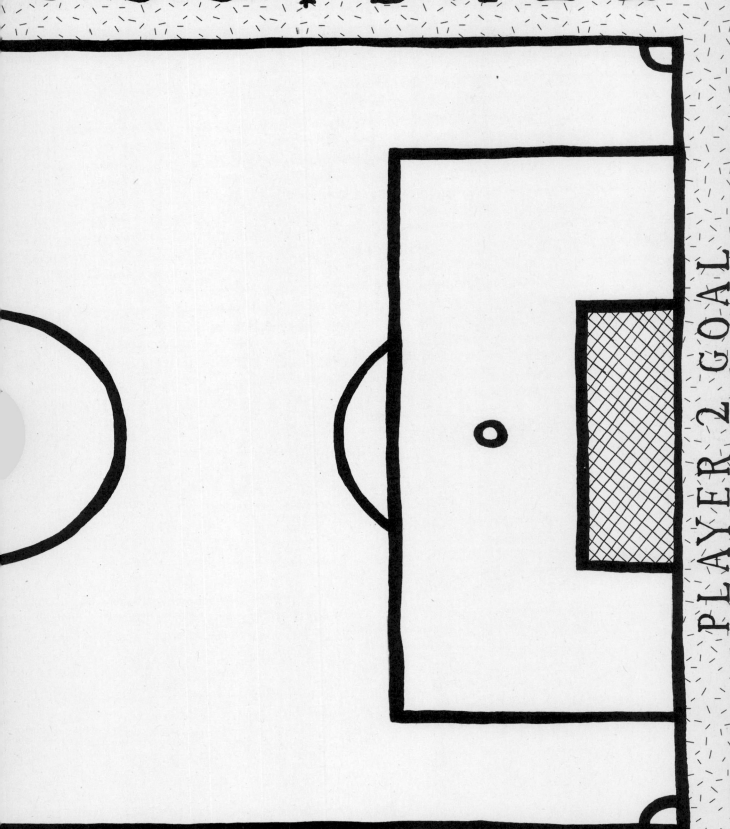

PLAYER 2 GOAL

The first player to score five goals is the winner! The ball MUST go into the criss-crossed area of the goal in order to count. Shooting from anywhere other than the 'O' is a foul and results in a point being given to your opponent!

TREASURE HUNT

HOW TO PLAY

1. Hold this page up so you can't see each other's pictures – no cheating!

   Count down, 'On your marks... Get set... Go!'. On 'Go', start searching for the objects listed on this page in your picture. When you find one, circle it.

2. The first player to find all the objects is the winner. If you think you have found all the objects, call out 'Treasure found!'. The other player can check your picture. If it turns out you have missed any, the other player automatically wins!!

YOU MUST FIND:

A bow   A pin

A flower   A teddy   A nest
               bear

A tennis   A watch   A pair of
racket   scissors

A rabbit   A peg

TREASURE HUNT

YOU MUST FIND:

A bow   A pin   A die

A flower

A teddy   A nest
bear

A tennis   A pair of
racket   scissors

A watch

A rabbit   A peg

HOW TO PLAY

1. Hold this page up so you can't see each other's pictures – no cheating!

Count down, 'On your marks... Get set...
2. Go!'. On 'Go', start searching for the objects listed on this page in your picture. When you find one, circle it.

3. The first player to find all the objects is the winner. If you think you have found all the objects, call out 'Treasure found!'. The other player can check your picture. If it turns out you have missed any, the other player automatically wins!!

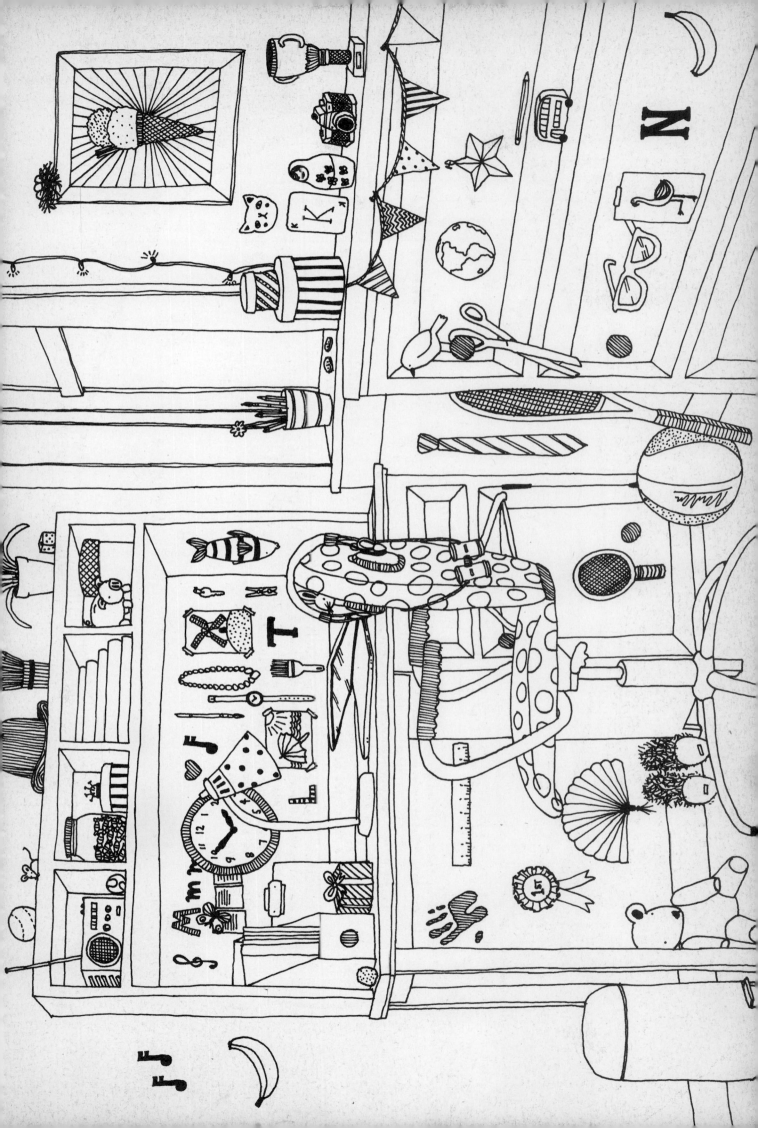

THE MIND-BL

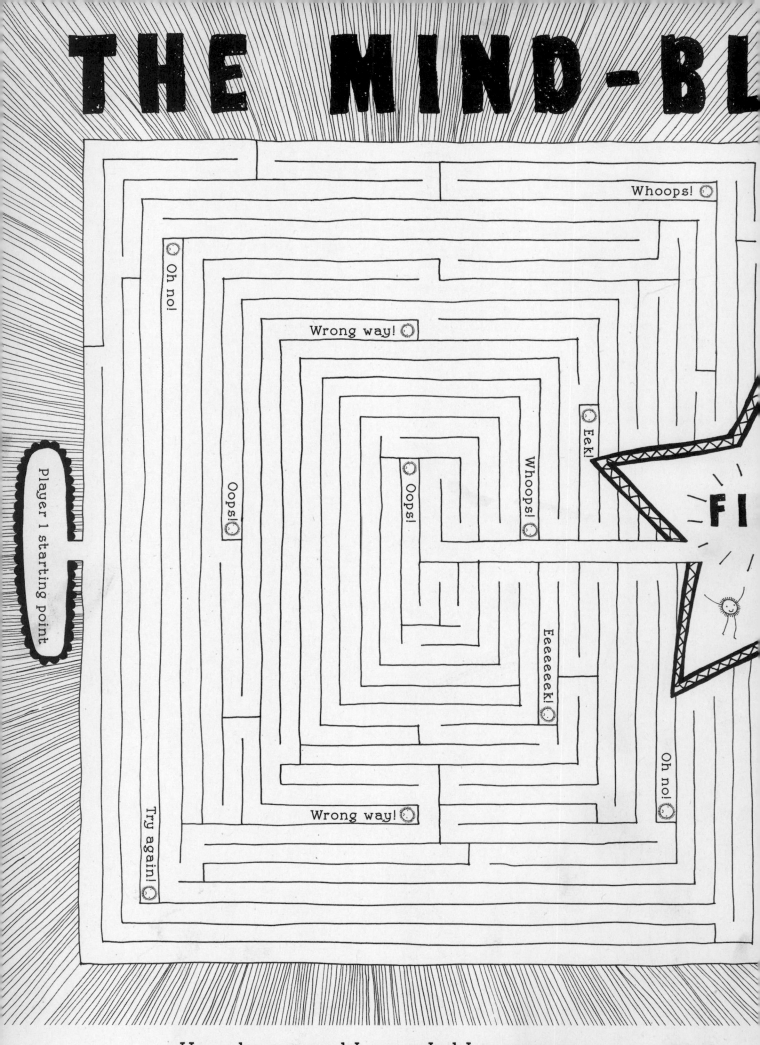

How to race through the maze . . .
Face each other at opposite sides of the book. See which player can get through the maze on their page and reach the centre first.

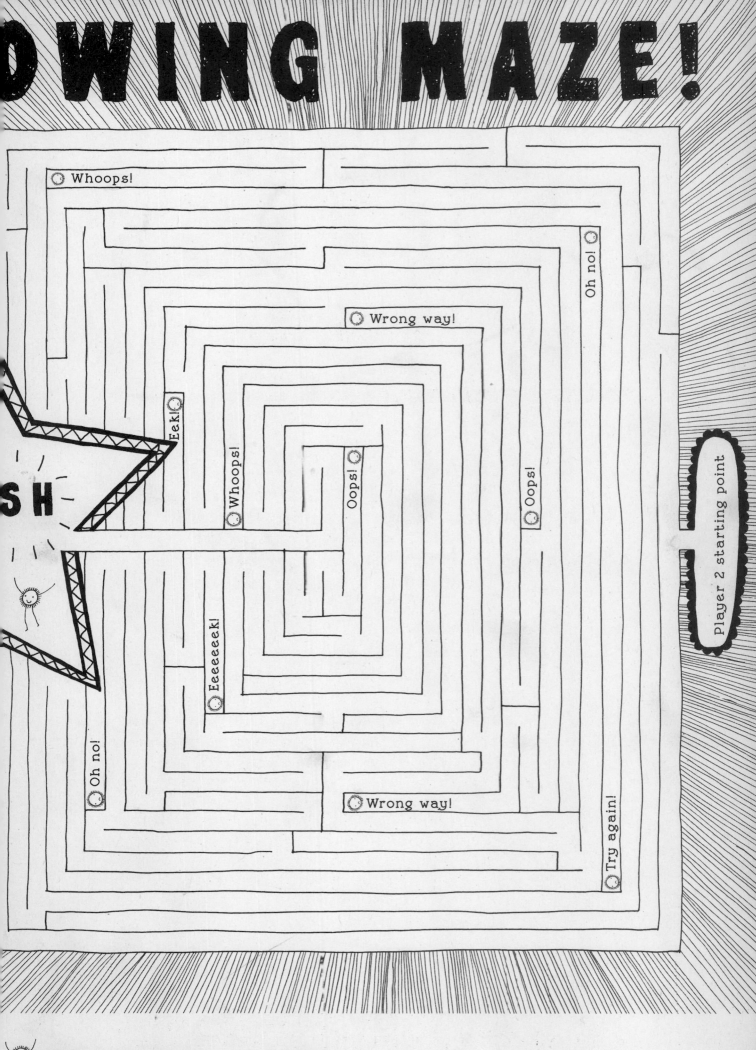

PLAY MORE
SQUARES
ON THIS PAGE

→

How to play . . .

Take turns to draw a single line to join any two
dots that are next to each other on the grid.
The lines can join the dots horizontally or
vertically (but not diagonally).

The player who draws the line that completes one
square earns one point and gets another turn.
Put your initials in that square.

The game ends when no more lines can be drawn,
and the player with the most points wins. This grid
is bigger than the first one, so you can score
more points!

Good luck!

PLAYER 1 STATS

Name _____

Age _____

Number of squares won

_____

PLAYER 2 STATS

Name _____

Age _____

Number of squares won

_____

The winner was _____ with ___ squares.

SAY WHAT YOU SEE - AGAIN!

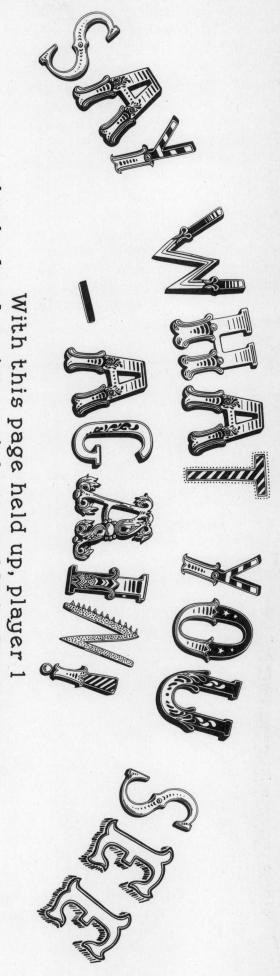

With this page held up, player 1 starts by drawing a picture on their drawing page.

Good work – but now the hard part!

Describe the shapes and lines that make up your picture, without saying what you have drawn. For example, if you drew a house you could describe it as a square with a triangle on top. Player 2 must try to draw a copy of it on their guessing page, just from the description.

No questions, and no guessing until the end!

To make it harder this time, set a timer and see if you can both complete your pictures in one minute.

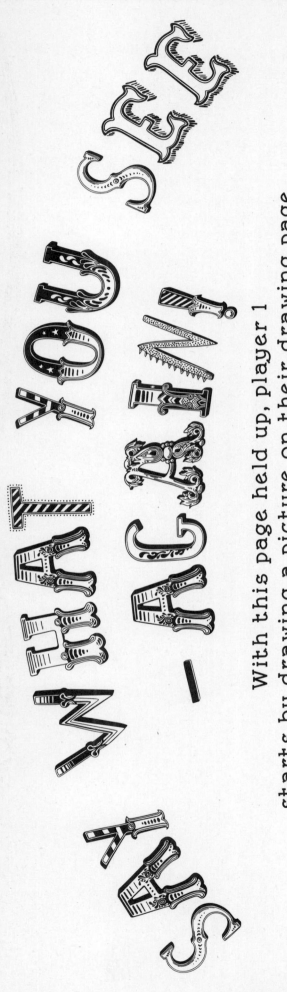

WHAT YOU SEE IS WHAT YOU AC-TU-AL-LY SAY

With this page held up, player 1 starts by drawing a picture on their drawing page.

Good work – but now the hard part!

Describe the shapes and lines that make up your picture, without saying what you have drawn. For example, if you drew a house you could describe it as a square with a triangle on top. Player 2 must try to draw a copy of it on their guessing page, just from the description.

No questions, and no guessing until the end!

To make it harder this time, set a timer and see if you can both complete your pictures in one minute.

Guessing page

Drawing page

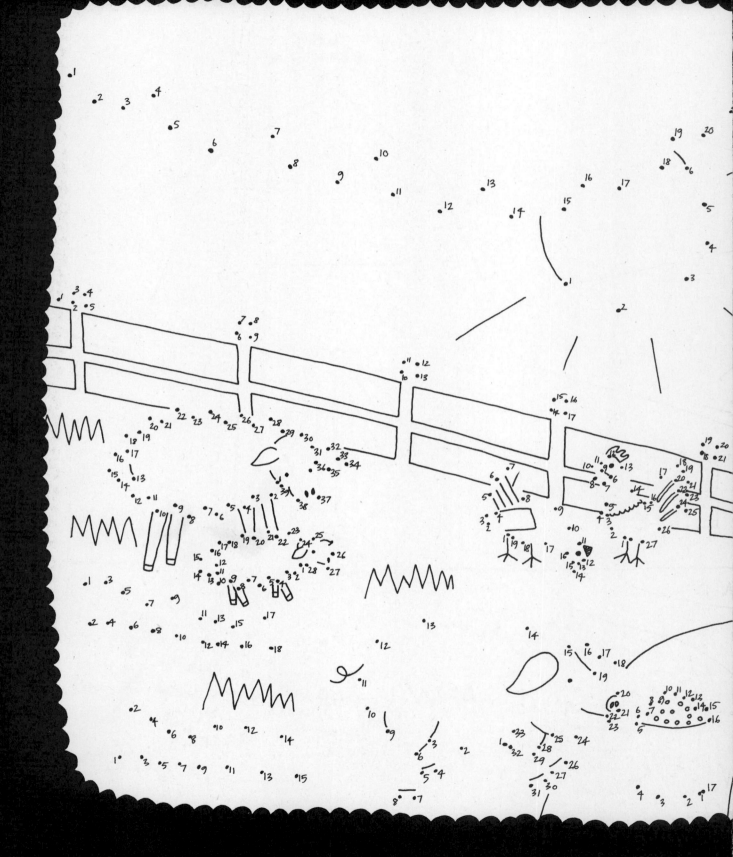

WHAT'S THE STORY? Part 2

PLAYER 1'S STORY

1 .... was a strange sort of

2 .... She lived in a

3 .... , for a start, and she was

also 4 .... , which made it hard to 5

.... She couldn't use a regular

6 .... so she had to

7 .... to school, 8 .... !

WORD KEY:

1. Female name
2. Noun
3. Noun
4. Adjective
5. Verb
6. Noun
7. Verb
8. Adverb (ending ...ly)

HOW IT WORKS . . .

Read through your story (silently!), and ask the other player for words to fill in the gaps (clues on the types of words you need are provided). Once you've both filled in all the gaps, take turns to read your story aloud, and see whose is the funniest.

WORD TYPES

VERB - a doing word - walk, cook, jump...
NOUN - a naming word - house, giraffe, river...
ADJECTIVE - a describing word - green, tall, strange...
ADVERB - describes the way an action happens - slowly, completely, gently...
EXCLAMATION - a short utterance - Gosh! Hurrah! Cripes!

PLAYER 2'S STORY

On a visit to the zoo, 1 .... went to see the 2 .... , which were his favourite animals. They weren't in their enclosure, though, and a 3 .... anteater told him to look in the café. He went to the café, 4 .... , a huge 5 .... and found them all 6 .... for him!" 7 .... !" he shouted, as they all sat down to 8 ....

WORD KEY:

1. Boy's name
2. Noun (plural)
3. Adjective
4. Adverb (ending ...ly)
5. Verb (ending ...ing)
6. Noun
7. Exclamation!
8. Verb

MANDALA DRAWING

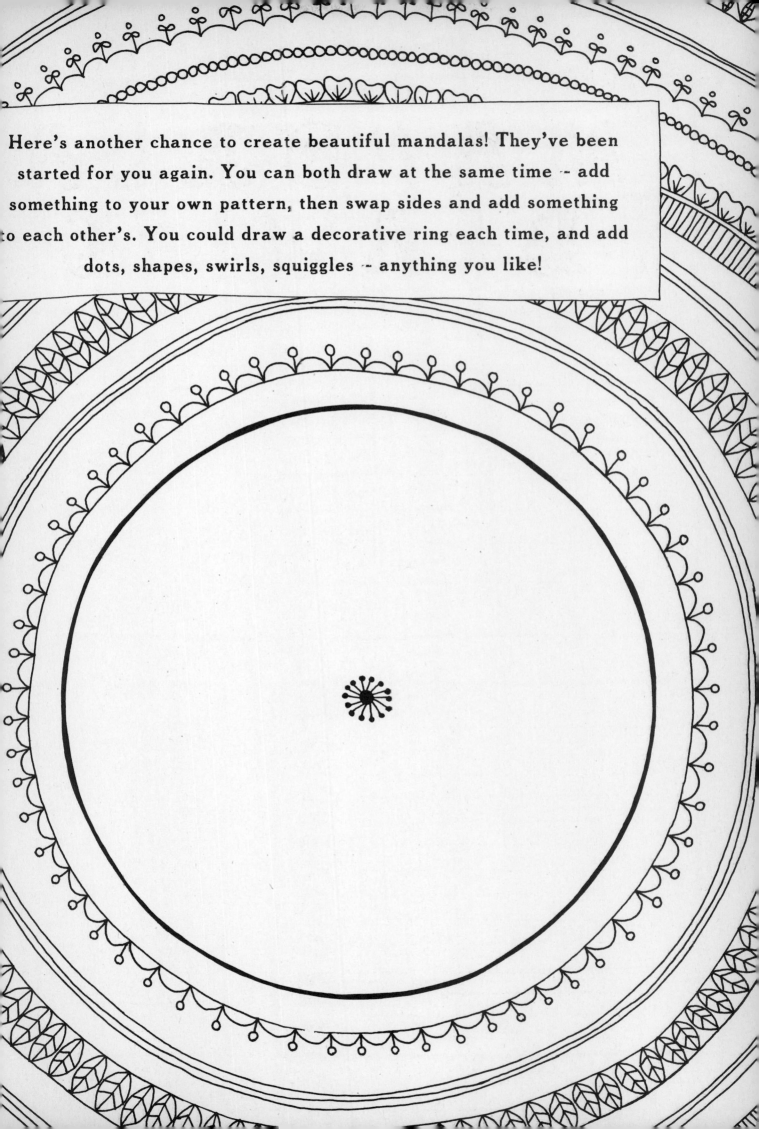

Here's another chance to create beautiful mandalas! They've been started for you again. You can both draw at the same time -- add something to your own pattern, then swap sides and add something to each other's. You could draw a decorative ring each time, and add dots, shapes, swirls, squiggles -- anything you like!

MAIN GRID

Draw your fleet on this grid.

	1	2	3	4	5	6	7	8	9	10	11	12
L												
K												
J												
I												
H												
G												
F												
E												
D												
C												
B												
A												

YOUR FLEET

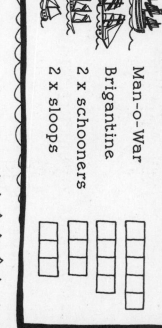

Man-o-War

Brigantine

2 x schooners

2 x sloops

TRACKING GRID

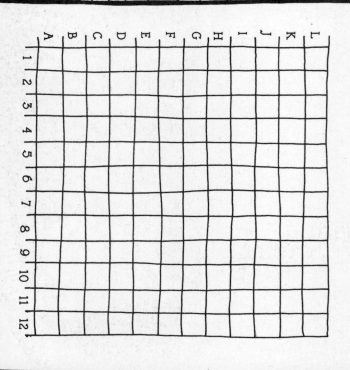

	1	2	3	4	5	6	7	8	9	10	11	12
L												
K												
J												
I												
H												
G												
F												
E												
D												
C												
B												
A												

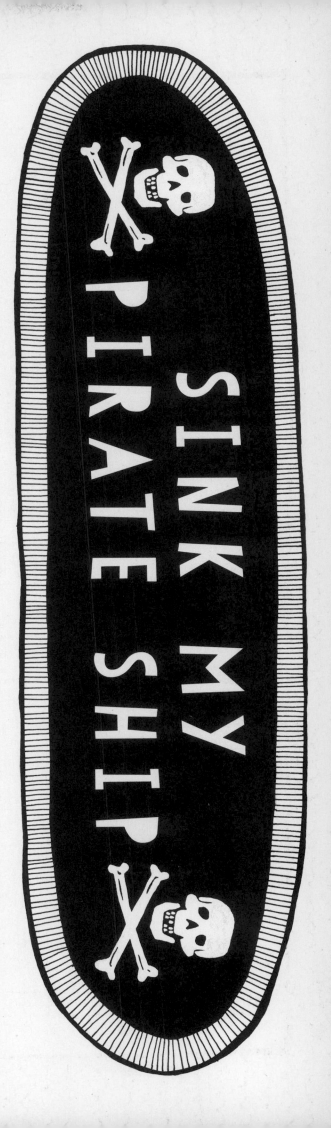

SINK MY PIRATE SHIP

HOW TO PLAY . . .

With this page held up, choose where you want each boat in your pirate fleet to be. Shade in the correct number of squares on the main grid for each boat, then you're ready to play.

Take turns in calling out a square from the grid (A3, D5, etc). If the other player has a boat on a square you call out, they should tell you that you've got a hit. Mark hits with a cross on your tracking grid, and misses with a dash. This will help you build a picture of where the other player's fleet is.

Once you've guessed all of the squares taken up by one boat, you have SUNK THE PIRATE SHIP — Arrr! When all of one player's boats have been sunk, the game is over and the other player wins.

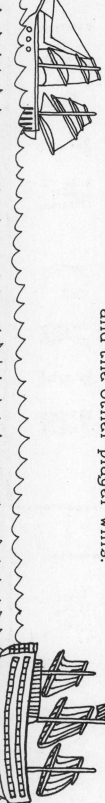

SINK MY PIRATE SHIP

HOW TO PLAY . . . .

With this page held up, choose where you want each boat in your pirate fleet to be. Shade in the correct number of squares on the main grid for each boat, then you're ready to play.

Take turns in calling out a square from the grid (A3, D5, etc). If the other player has a boat on a square you call out, they should tell you that you've got a hit. Mark hits with a cross on your tracking grid, and misses with a dash. This will help you build a picture of where the other player's fleet is.

Once you've guessed all of the squares taken up by one boat, you have SUNK THE PIRATE SHIP – Arrrr! When all of one player's boats have been sunk, the game is over and the other player wins.

YOUR FLEET

Man-o-War

Brigantine

2 x schooners

2 x sloops

TRACKING GRID

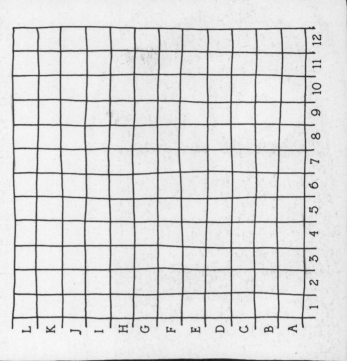

L
K
J
I
H
G
F
E
D
C
B
A

1 2 3 4 5 6 7 8 9 10 11 12

MAIN GRID

Draw your fleet on this grid.

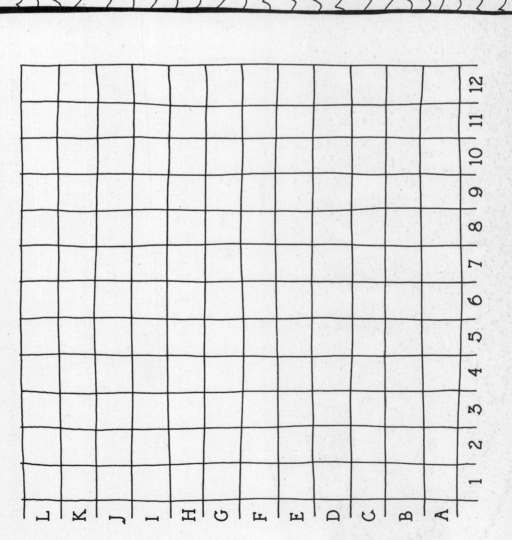

L
K
J
I
H
G
F
E
D
C
B
A

1 2 3 4 5 6 7 8 9 10 11 12

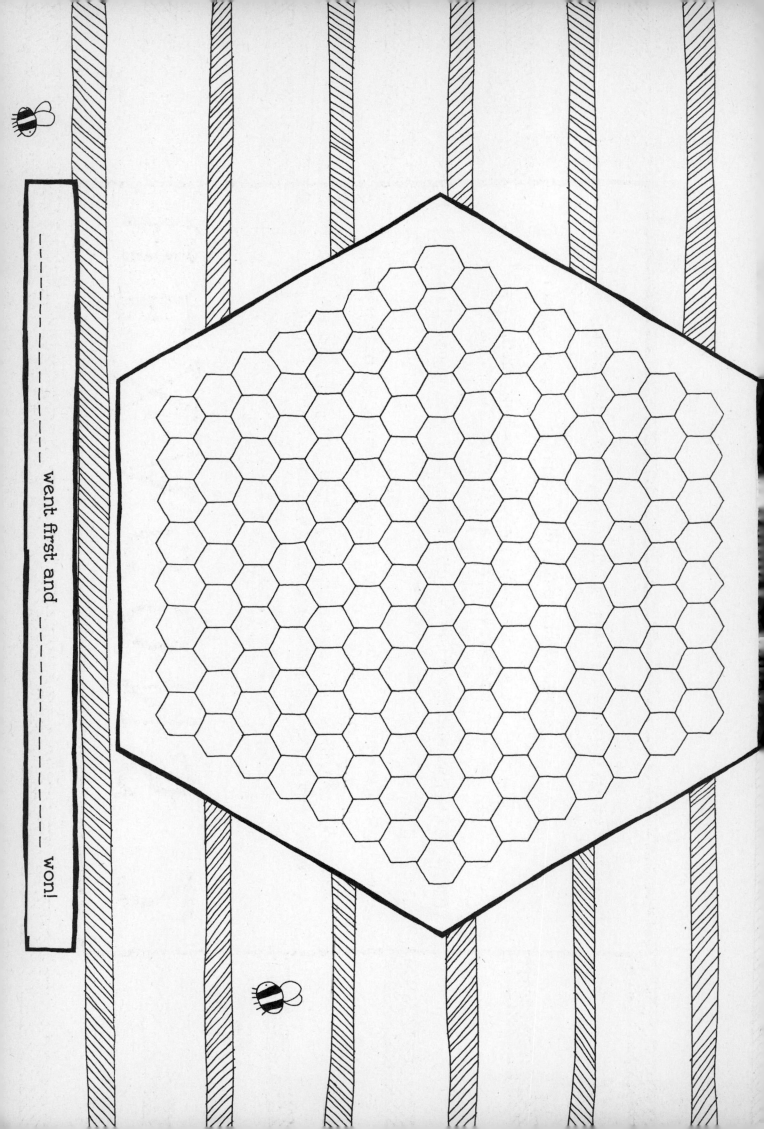

_____ went first and _____ won!

HEXAGONS 2

HOW TO PLAY

Each player should choose a coloured pencil to use for the game. Take turns to fill in one 'cell' of the board at a time with your colour.

The aim is to colour cells next to each other to create one of three types of connection:

1 A ring, which is a continuous loop with at least one cell in the middle.

2 A fork, which connects three edges of the board (the corners don't count as an edge).

3 A bridge, which connects any two of the corners.

To up the stakes, see if you can complete the game within three minutes...

MY SCORE WAS:

MY LIST OF WORDS FOUND:

As before, take turns calling out letters and writing them in the grids. The aim is to arrange the letters as you write them down to make as many words as possible . . . .

Once your grids are full, mark down all the words you can find, and work out your scores. You get points for words in a vertical or horizontal row (not diagonals):

6-letter word ~ Wowee, 15 points!
5-letter word ~ Whew, well done! 10 points!
4-letter word ~ Good effort, have 5 points.
3-letter word ~ Not bad, have 2 points.
2-letter word ~ Alright, 1 point.

This time, once your grids are full, you have just three minutes to find all the words!

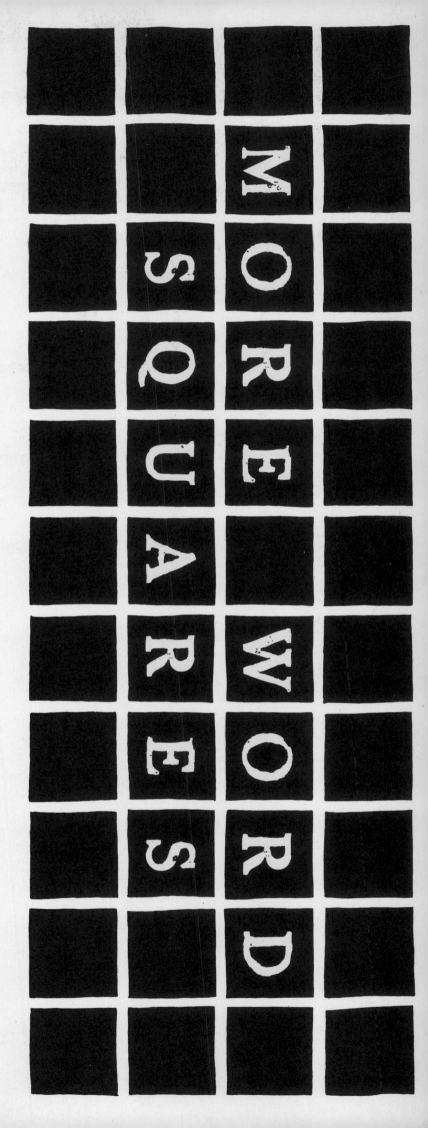

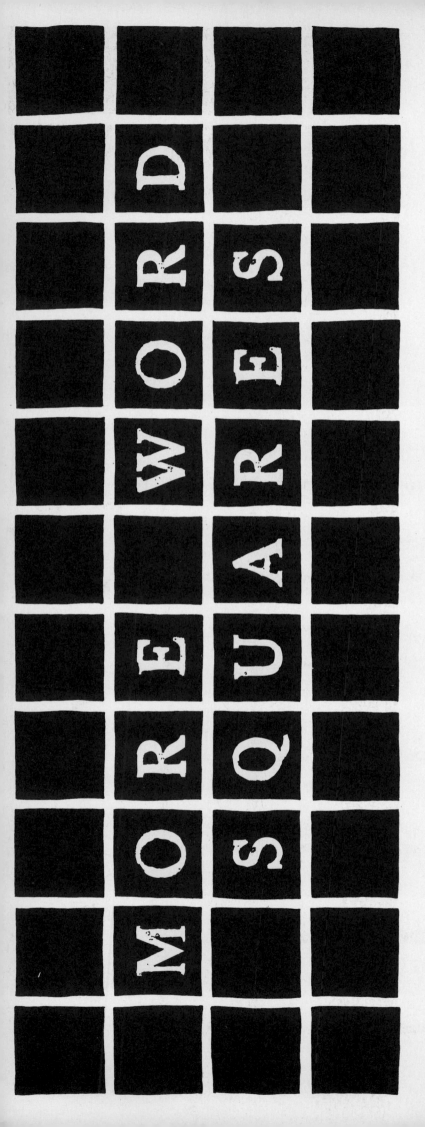

As before, take turns calling out letters and writing them in the grids. The aim is to arrange the letters as you write them down to make as many words as possible . . . .

Once your grids are full, mark down all the words you can find, and work out your scores. You get points for words in a vertical or horizontal row (not diagonals):

6-letter word -- Wowee, 15 points!
5-letter word -- Whew, well done! 10 points!
4-letter word -- Good effort, have 5 points.
3-letter word -- Not bad, have 2 points.
2-letter word -- Alright, 1 point.

This time, once your grids are full, you have just three minutes to find all the words!

MY LIST OF WORDS FOUND:

MY SCORE WAS:

SQUIGGLE

Run out of ideas for new pictures again? No problem!

Do a quick squiggle in the middle of the frame,
then turn the book around.

Started by -------

Completed by -------

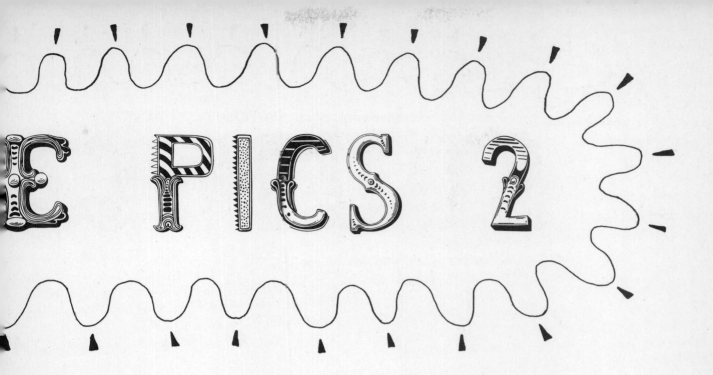

PICS 2

Now that the other player has started your drawing, you can see what you think it looks like and turn it into a complete work of art.

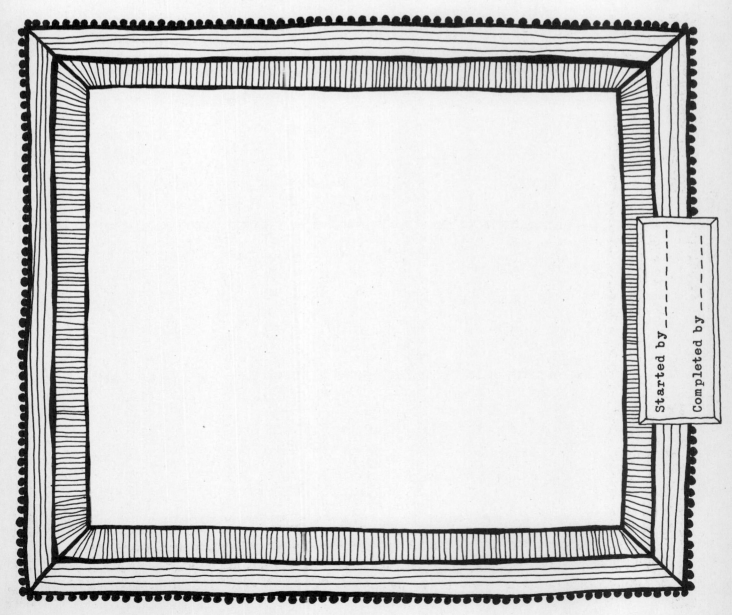

Started by _ _ _ _ _ _

Completed by _ _ _ _

MY TOTAL CATEGORIES SCORE WAS:--------

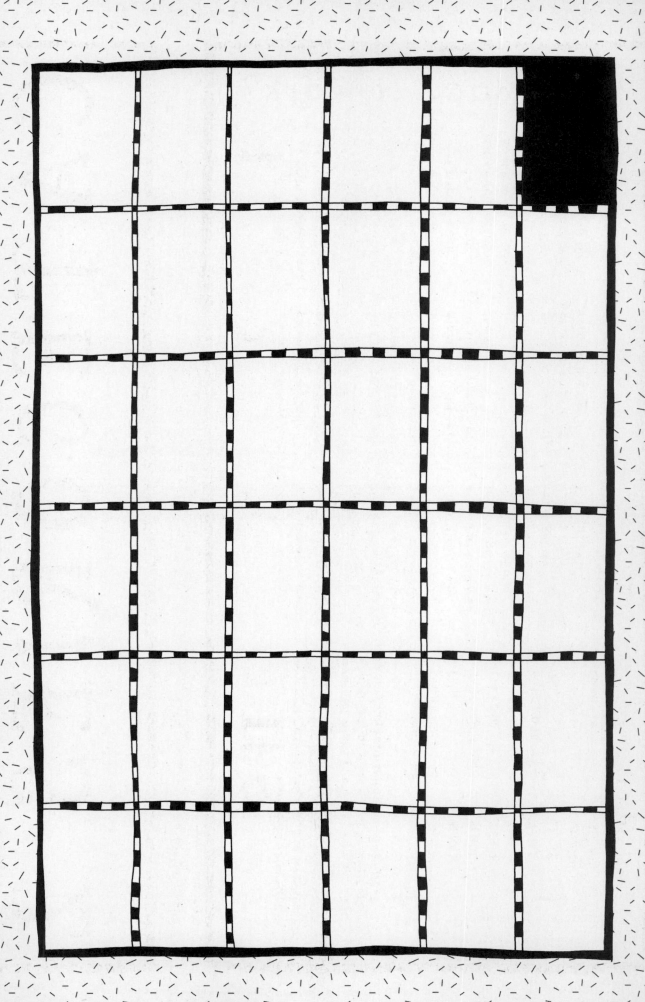

CATEGORIES 2

How does it work?

1. This time you can choose your own categories and keyword. Write a category at the top of each column Then, choose a five-letter keyword and write it down the left side of each player's grid, so that each letter is at the start of one row. Both your grids need to have the same keyword and categories, in the same order.

2. Hold up this page, set a timer for four minutes – then you're ready!

In each square, write a word that fits under the category at the top of the column and starts with the letter at the beginning of the row.

The game is finished when the time is up, or when one player fills their grid.

3. Compare your answers and make sure you agree the words are OK (no made-up words!). You get no points for words that you both wrote down, but one point per word that only you thought of. If you filled the whole grid you get five bonus points.

The player with the most points wins!

TIPS:

You can choose any five categories, and any five-letter keyword (as long as it does not contain repeated letters – and it's best to avoid Q, X and Z, unless you want a BIG challenge, or a long game!). Here are some suggestions to get you started:

Categories:	Keywords:
– Cities	– REACH
– Birds	– BENCH
– Flowers	– BLADE
– Types of food	– GLIDE
– Vehicles	– BENDY
– Body parts	– TABLE
– Toys	– BEARS
– Insects	– LAUGH
– Buildings	– HOUND

CATEGORIES 2

1. This time you can choose your own categories and keyword. Write a category at the top of each column. Then, choose a five-letter keyword and write it down the left side of each player's grid, so that each letter is at the start of one row. Both your grids need to have the same keyword and categories, in the same order.

2. Hold up this page, set a timer for four minutes – then you're ready!

In each square, write a word that fits under the category at the top of the column, and starts with the letter at the beginning of the row.

The game is finished when the time is up, or when one player fills their grid.

3. Compare your answers and make sure you agree the words are OK (no made-up words!). You get no points for words that you and the other player both wrote down, but one point per word that only you thought of. If you filled the whole grid you get five bonus points.

The player with the most points wins!

TIPS:
You can choose any five categories, and any five-letter keyword (as long as it does not contain repeated letters – and it's best to avoid Q, X and Z, unless you want a BIG challenge, or a long game!). Here are some suggestions to get you started:

Categories:
- Cities
- Birds
- Types of food
- Flowers
- Vehicles
- Body parts
- Toys
- Insects
- Buildings

Keywords:
- REACH
- BENCH
- BLADE
- GLIDE
- BENDY
- TABLE
- BEARS
- LAUGH
- HOUND

MY TOTAL CATEGORIES SCORE WAS: _ _ _ _ _ _

TAG-TEAM DRAWING

Make a super-speedy sketch with another game of tag-team drawing, against the clock . . .
Set a timer for two minutes - when it starts, player 1 does a quick, simple doodle, then rotates the paper 90 degrees. Player 2 then adds to the doodle and rotates the paper another 90 degrees. Keep taking turns until you're out of time... Keep it quick!!

HOW TO PLAY:

One player plays with black dots, the other plays with white dots.

Take turns connecting your dots, one line at a time. You can connect up or across (not diagonally), and you can only connect dots of your own colour. You cannot cross a line that has already been drawn.

The aim is to connect the dots in your colour to make a continuous line (or pipe) between the shorter sides of your grid.

LAYER

● Black dot player's name _ _ _ _ _ _ _ _ _ _ _ _ _ _ _ _ _ _

○ White dot player's name _ _ _ _ _ _ _ _ _ _ _ _ _ _ _ _ _ _

◄ - - - - - White dot player joins side to side - - - ►

▲ Black dot player joins up or down ▼

The winner was _

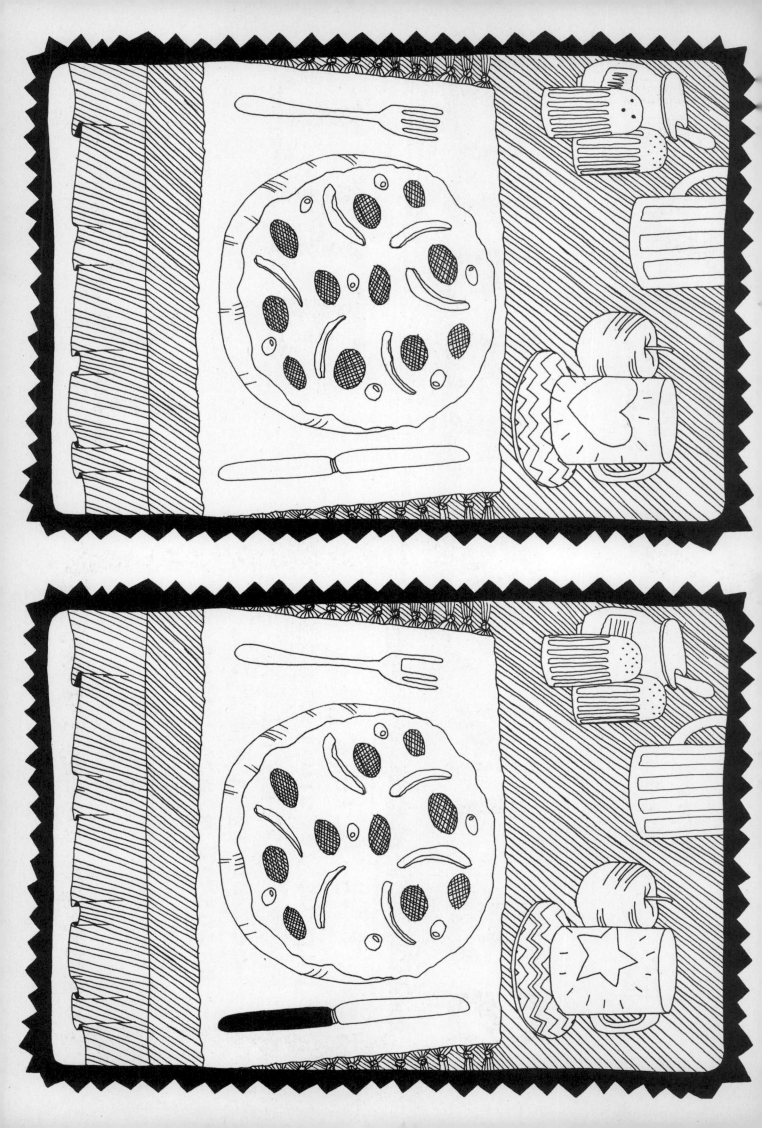

SPOT THE DIFFERENCES RACE

Race each other to find the ten differences between these pictures — circle them as you find them. The first player to find all ten, wins.

Hold this page up — and no peeking!

SPOT THE DIFFERENCES

Race each other to find the ten differences between these pictures — circle them as you find them.

The first player to find all ten, wins.

RACE

Hold this page up — and no peeking!

PICTURE

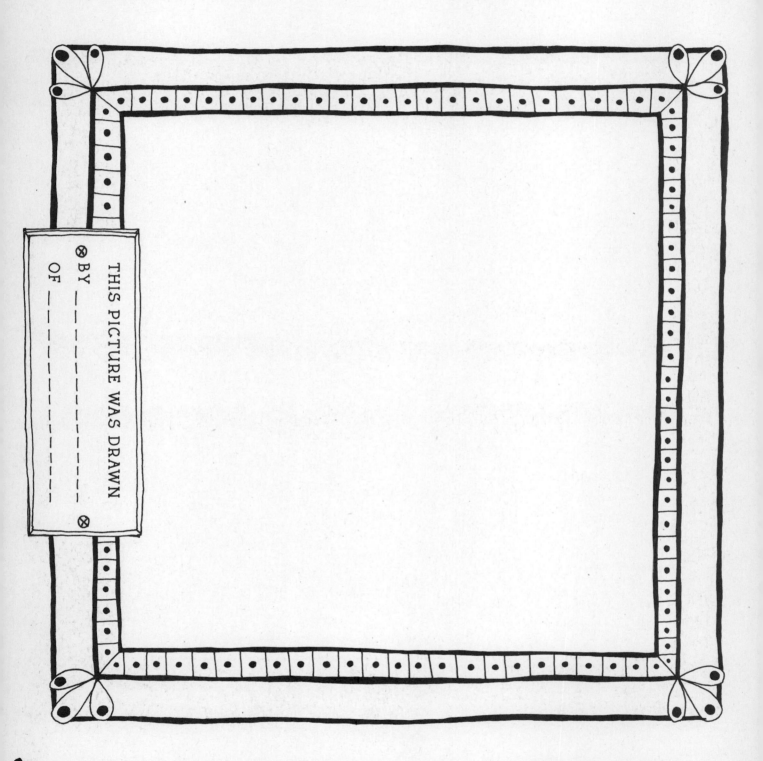

THIS PICTURE WAS DRAWN

⊗ BY
_ _ _ _ _ _ _ _

OF
_ _ _ _ _ _ _ _

Another chance to draw a portrait of your fellow-player. HOWEVER, this time you must hold the pencil in your non-dominant hand.

PERFECT 2

THIS PICTURE WAS DRAWN
⊗ BY - - - - - - - - - -
OF - - - - - - - -

Yes, if you're right-handed, it's time to try with the left, and if you're left-handed, swap to the right. Tricky...

MORE SPROUTS!

Sprouts is like a game of dot-to-dots,
but with a twist . . .

Here's how it works:

Starting with the three dots on the opposite page,
take turns to draw a line to connect two dots
(or the line may start and end on the same dot).
You should also draw a new dot somewhere on
your new line.

Lines cannot cross, and each dot can only have
three lines sprouting out of it. Eventually, it will
become impossible to draw a new line without
crossing an existing one -- the last player to
draw a line wins!

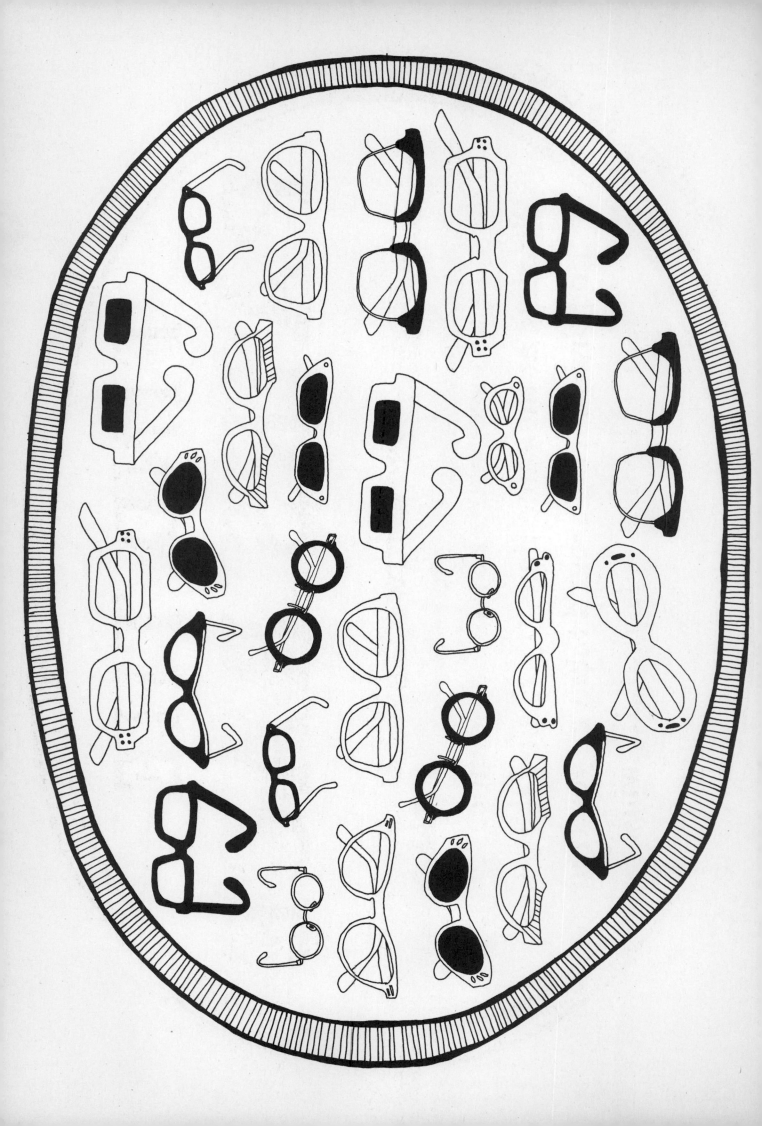

FIND THE PAIRS RACE

How it works:

Hidden in this scene are 12 pairs of identical glasses.

Starting at the same time, try to find the pairs and draw a ring around them as you find them – the first to find all 12, wins!

FIND THE PAIRS RACE

How it works:

Hidden in this scene are 12 pairs of identical glasses.

Starting at the same time, try to find the pairs

and draw a ring around them as you find

them – the first to find all 12, wins!

Hold up this page

MIRROR DRAWING 2

drew this picture

Another chance to play artist and student... The artist begins drawing
in their frame, while their student must exactly mirror what they are
drawing (at the same time), to create a perfect mirror image.

MIRROR DRAWING 2

_____ drew this picture

Another chance to play artist and student... The artist begins drawing in their frame, while their student must exactly mirror what they are drawing (at the same time), to create a perfect mirror image.

Me completed this book on

Hold this page up to a mirror and then write your completion date below (but the writing has to be back-to-front, too).